HOW TO MAKE
$1000 A WEEK AS
A NOTARY PUBLIC

VANESSA TERRY

Author, Vanessa Terry

As a mother of three, originally from New York and currently residing in Virginia, I have been a notary public and practicing as a signing agent since 2014. I obtained my commission in Henrico, VA, as I wanted to find an income stream that would not only give me the time freedom to attend my children's soccer games on the weekends or after school programs during the week, but I also needed it to produce a full-time income to provide for my family.

When I began as a notary public, I did not have another notary or training program to teach me the ropes and I learned everything from internet searches or trial and error. Six years later, I earn well over $1000 a week with consistent clients and have the time freedom I never knew was possible from a career that I **NEVER** knew existed. I also never have to miss my children's sporting events or birthday's either!

I started Notary2Notary to help teach others how to create a sustainable business as a Notary Public/Signing agent and produce similar and even greater results. I love being able to attend events with my family and not having to call a manager or boss to request time off.

Notary2Notary is about helping people gain time freedom while earning sustainable income!

Preface

"How to Make $1000 A Week As A Notary Public" is designed as a guide to teach new and existing notaries how to set up a notary business and make it profitable. The book is based on the Notary2Notary online training program (www.notary2notary.com). While reviewing the information in this book, it is important that you check with you own State Notary Commissioning Office as laws change all the time and you want to make sure you are working as a notary within the current legalities. This book is not intended to provide legal or tax advice and is simply an instructional guide to help you get started building a successful notary business today.

The title of this book says you can make $1000 a week and that is true, but you can also earn much more than that. Now I never guarantee results, but I have been in this business long enough to know that the system works if you work it! I chose $1000 a week as a starting point because it is achievable, if you use all the principles presented in this book, complete the training through the Notary2Notary program and spend time investing in your business. The sky is the limit on what you will be able to earn! There are notaries who earn upwards of $6000-$15,000 a month and that can very easily be you. Take your time and learn the material to ensure you understand each step necessary to build your business. In addition, by joining the Notary2Notary program you can ask questions as you go along and interact with other beginning and experienced notaries in our online N2N Facebook group: www.facebook.com/groups/notary2notary.

As we say at Notary2Notary, "HAPPY SIGNING!"

NOTARY II NOTARY

CHAPTERS

CHAPTER 1
WHAT IS A NOTARY PUBLIC AND WHAT ARE THE RESPONSIBILITIES?

A notary public is a public officer constituted by law to serve the public whose main functions are to administer oaths and affirmations, take affidavits and statutory declarations, witness and authenticate the execution of certain classes of documents, take acknowledgments of deeds and other conveyances, provide exemplifications and notarial copies, and perform certain other official acts depending on the jurisdiction. Any such act is known as a **notarization.**

A notary acts as an official, unbiased witness to the identity and signature of the person who comes before the notary for a specific purpose. The person may be taking an oath, giving oral or written testimony, or signing or acknowledging his or her signature on a legal document. In each case, the notary attests that certain formalities have been observed.

The main responsibility of a notary public is to be as certain as possible that the person appearing before them is indeed the person in the presented forms of identification such as their state-issued driver's license or passport. Identification documents **must** have a photo of the signer on them as well, to authenticate verification of identity. Some states do allow you to notarize documents without the signer presenting a valid form of identification if you confirm that you personally know the signer. Be sure to read your state's notary handbook before using the latter as a form of identity verification.

In some states, notaries are also allowed to perform marriages, but you want to be sure to check with your state's commission to be compliant with your state's laws.

It is very important to understand and comply with the law that prohibits notary publics from providing legal advice. There will be times when clients may ask legal questions and you must know when it is permissible to answer or when it is best to refer them to consult with a lawyer. You also never want to provide legal documents to a signer such as if a signer asks for you to give them a Power of Attorney to use. You want to encourage them to contact an attorney or even research online for one they would like to use. If you provide certain legal documents to be signed you are providing legal advice and that can cause issues for you in the future.

Failure to comply with your state's standards can result in a revocation of your notary commission, fines, lawsuits and even criminal charges.

History of Notary Publics in America

In Colonial America, only persons of high moral character were appointed as notary publics to certify and keep documents safe. Their contributions to colonial life are largely seen as the reason American business became a huge success. For example, in colonial times notaries were invaluable to trans-Atlantic commerce, as parties on both sides depended on them to be honest third parties in reporting damage or loss to a ship's cargo. While notaries were held in very high regard during this time, life for notaries in early America was anything but easy. Some were even killed for their involvement in authenticating official documents and recordkeeping as conflicting factions fought for control of the New World. The Colony of New Haven (Connecticut) appointed the first notary public in America in 1639.

Women in America were prohibited from becoming notaries. U.S. Supreme Court Justice Oliver Wendell Holmes Jr. held that since there was no record of women holding the office in England, it could not be affirmed that women were capable of being notaries. Today, more than two-thirds of America's notaries are women.

Notary Publics Today

As a notary, you can build your business with numerous tiers of work such as conducting marriages (depending on state), standard notarizations for your everyday people (GNW), real estate transactions as a signing agent, building relationships with lawyers and estate planners for purposes of notarizing wills, trusts and powers of attorney, conducting E-Notarizations and even completing some popular non-notary work like fingerprinting. Preference depends on what you decide is best for you, and I recommend trying them all out in the beginning to get an understanding of what a notary public can legally do in your state.

Many people think that the notary industry is a small trade that is dying off with technology but that is far from true. Many people also think that it is going to be an elderly woman meeting with them or that they can only get documents notarized at funeral homes. This is far from truth!

Notaries around the United States are various demographics and backgrounds. Anyone who is a United States citizen, 18 or over, who can pass a background check and exam (in some states), can become a commissioned notary public. We have students in our online training from varying ages all of the country who have successfully built their notary business and have been able to quit their full time job. Be sure to check out our student reviews on our YouTube Channel: @NOTARY2NOTARYUSA www.youtube.com/notary2notaryusa

Notaries who run their own businesses full time can make more than your average entry level careers and even many upper-management positions. The key to having a successful notary business is knowing your trade and always conducting notarizations in excellence. **Remember that this is a business. Be sure to treat it as such!**

CHAPTER 2
HOW TO BECOME A COMMISSIONED & INSURED NOTARY PUBLIC

The **VERY** first thing that you need to do is apply for your notary commission with your Secretary of State/Commonwealth's/Notary Commissioning Office. Different states have varying requirements as to what you will need to provide or do to obtain your commission. Virginia is a state where you simply complete an application and pay a small application fee. The courts will then run a criminal background check and if there are no felony convictions on your record, you will be commissioned as a notary public. However, in California, Colorado, Connecticut, Hawaii, Louisiana, Maine, Montana, Nebraska, New York, North Carolina, Oregon and Utah you will have to take an exam in order to obtain your notary Commission. The state will refer you to either a training they provide or an outside vendor that provides the state specific training needed to pass the exam. Also, a quick note, do not count yourself out even if you have a criminal record. Every state is different as far as what they will allow, and I have a few students in my training that I know of that were approved for their notary commission with a criminal record. Many times, in life, we count ourselves out of opportunities because are afraid that we may be denied or rejected but I encourage you to try anyway. Give it a shot and the worst thing that can happen is your application is denied. But the best thing that can happen, is you build a six-figure notary business and enjoy time and financial freedom. I think that is worth the shot.

Be sure to read and follow your state's notary handbook. Every state has a notary handbook that explains what a notary can do legally and what is prohibited. Following the handbook and applicable laws is extremely important, as violations can not only cause you to lose your commission but can have monetary consequences.

Below are links to a few notary handbooks in various states.

Virginia:
https://www.commonwealth.virginia.gov/media/governorvirginiagov/secretary-of-the-commonwealth/pdf/2017-December-15-revised-Handbook-.pdf

California:

https://notary.cdn.sos.ca.gov/forms/notary-handbook-2019.pdf

Texas:
https://www.sos.state.tx.us/statdoc/edinfo.shtml

While you are waiting for your commission to be issued you can do a few things that will prepare you to start accepting clients immediately.

1. Decide if you want to use your current cell phone number or establish a new line (Remember any new expenses you incur can be used a deduction for tax purposes.) or you can set up a Google Voice number which sets up a cloud version phone number that rings directly to your cellular device using a different number. With Google Voice, you can also set up voicemail, send and receive text messages and review call history. Be careful when setting up a Google Voice number, as you want to make sure the calls and texts are actually coming through and going out. I recommend just using your current number or adding a new line.

   Expect to receive phone calls from all different kinds of numbers, even out of the country numbers. Excluding out of the country numbers, you will need to answer every phone call in order to grow your notary business, as it will be more than likely your potential clients on the other end of that line. You may receive restricted calls as well that you can answer at your own discretion.

2. You can also start setting up your credit card processing platforms as well. There are various forms of payment methods available

with today's increasing technology. I recommend setting up an account for the following:

CASHAPP https://cash.app/	**ZELLE** https://www.zellepay.com/
VENMO https://venmo.com/	**SQUARE** https://squareup.com/us/en or **PAYPAL HERE** https://us.paypal-here.com/

Each of these companies are free to create an account with and they take a small percentage of your sales to cover the credit card processing fee.

You will find that people usually do not have cash and would prefer to pay with one of these methods. Versus sending them to an ATM which is not the best customer service and takes more time, **you are** prepared to accept any form of payment (excluding checks, which we only recommend accepting from Signing, Title and Real Estate Companies for closings you conduct.)

Upon confirmation of approval of licensure as a notary public, you will receive your notary certificate which looks similar to one of these:

NOTARY I.D. NO.
1332549

COMMISSION NO.
FF 960389

STATE OF FLORIDA

Executive Department

I, Rick Scott, Governor of Florida, by virtue of the authority vested in me
by the Constitution and Laws of this State,
do hereby commission

Ann Marino

to be

NOTARY PUBLIC

in and for the State of Florida
from March 2, 2016 through March 1, 2020 and in the
Name of the People of the State of Florida to have, hold and exercise the said office and
all the powers and responsibilities appertaining thereto, and to receive the privileges
and emoluments thereof in accordance with the law,
In Testimony Whereof, I do hereunto set my hand and cause to be affixed the
Great Seal of the State, Tallahassee, Florida.

Governor

Secretary of State

NNAF

State of California

SECRETARY OF STATE

I, ALEX PADILLA, Secretary of State, in the name and by the authority of the People of the State of California, do appoint and commission

WILLIAM S. CADEMY

Notary Public

of the State of California

Commission Number: 2104835

Term commencing March 28, 2015 and ending March 27, 2019 with the principal place of business in the county of SAN DIEGO.

IN WITNESS WHEREOF, I execute this certificate and affix the GREAT SEAL of the State of California this 24th day of March 2015.

Secretary of State

Commonwealth of Virginia

To all to Whom these Presents Shall Come – Greeting:
Know Ye that our Governor, by virtue of the authority vested in him
by law, has appointed and does hereby commission
Tawanda S Walker
a Notary Public for the Commonwealth at Large,
subject to qualification in accordance with the Law in the Circuit Court
of the City of Norfolk, to serve term of four years

Given under my hand and under the Lesser Seal of the Commonwealth, at Richmond
May 9 in the year
Two thousand and sixteen
And in the two hundred fortieth year of the Commonwealth

By the Governor

Governor

Secretary of the Commonwealth

This Commission Expires: April 30, 2020

Notary Registration Number - 7519783

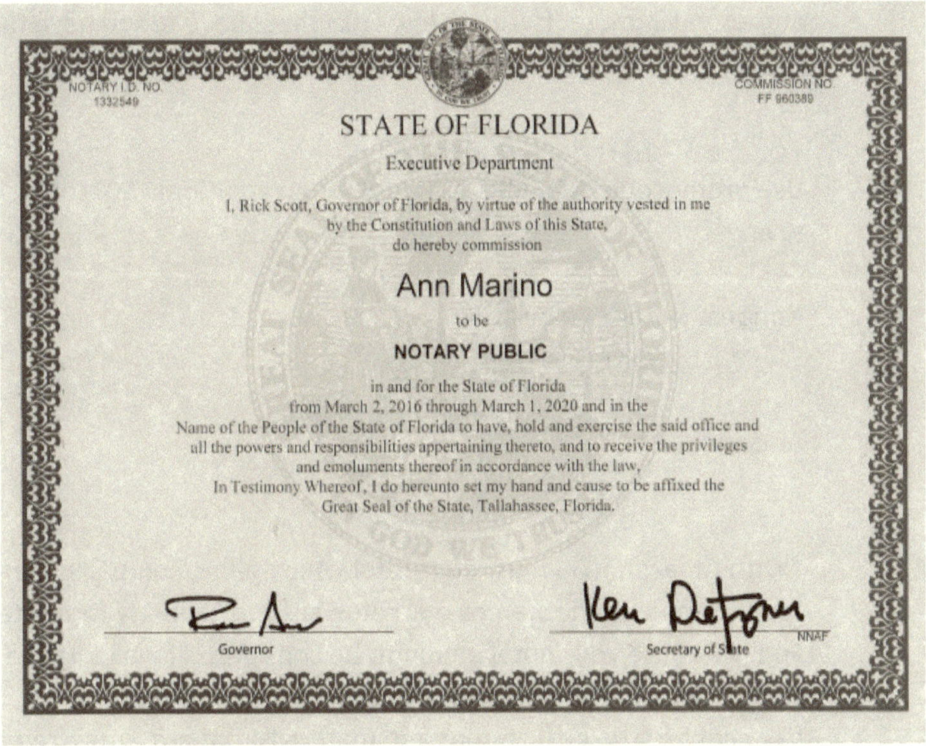

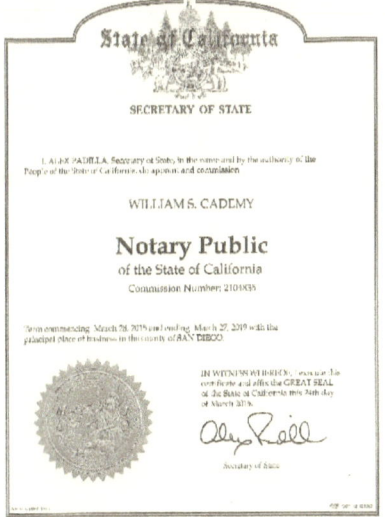

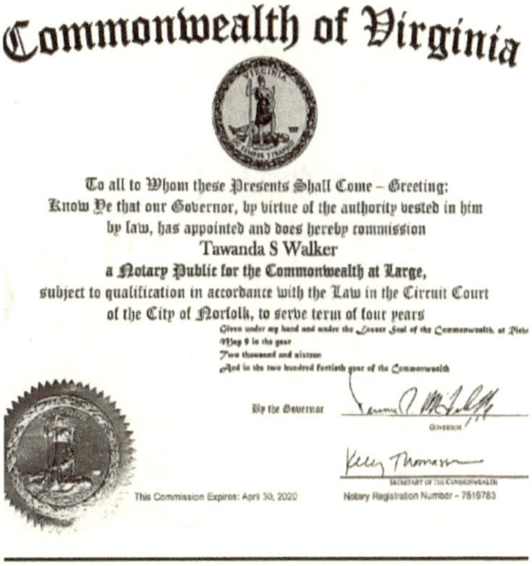

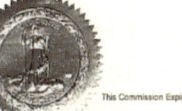

Once you have been sworn in by the clerk at your local courthouse, you are ready to order your notary stamp and supplies. There are many companies that offer supplies for notaries including stamps, embossers, certificates, notary journals and so much more. Here are few links that I have found have the quickest shipping and the best rates:

WWW.ALLSTATENOTARYSUPPLIES.COM
Use promocode: NOTARY2NOTARY for an additional 10% off savings!

National Notary Association
WWW.NATIONALNOTARY.ORG

Amazon
www.amazon.com

*With Amazon, you must be careful which seller/company you order from as some stamps marketed are not properly formatted and will cause your notarization to be considered invalid. In the Notary2Notary training course (www.notary2notary.com), we have links to the best stamps and materials that are formatted correctly. You can also visit the Notary2Notary's YouTube Channel to watch a short video with this information:
https://www.youtube.com/channel/UChtRcuc0V8BfDKazh6mwcSQ

When deciding on which supplies to purchase, you want to make sure that you have the basics:

1. Notary Stamp/Embosser
2. Attachable Certificates
3. Notary Journal
4. Fingerprint Pad (if applicable)
5. Pens (Be sure to purchase black and blue pens)

THE GREAT STAMP VS EMBOSSER DEBATE

One of the most important part of notarizing a document is affixing your notary seal. This seal is verification that a commissioned notary public did in fact verify identities of said signers and witnessed the presenting signatures. The notary seal can be used with either an Ink based Stamp or an Ink/Ink-less Embosser. This specification is determined by your state and must be adhered to for the notarization to be valid. A notary seal will look like one of the following:

Stamps:

Embossers:

The term "Notary seal" is often used interchangeably with stamp and embosser.

Notary seal stamps are inked rubber stamps that imprint state required information — usually the Notary Public's name, state of commission and date of commission expiration. Notary stamps are usually rectangular or circular, but some states require a round stamp. Each state maintains its own requirement for the stamps used by its notaries.

Notary Seal Requirement for Each State

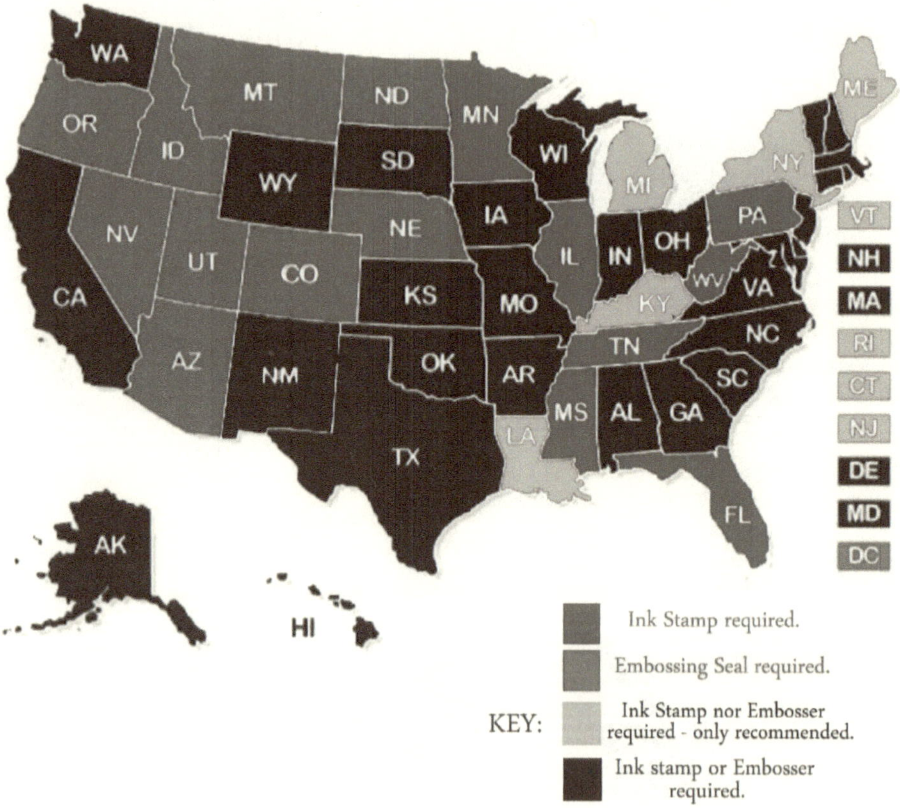

KEY:
- Ink Stamp required.
- Embossing Seal required.
- Ink Stamp nor Embosser required - only recommended.
- Ink stamp or Embosser required.

The above map gives you an overview of the requirements of your state, but each state has specific constraints attached to their requirements. Please, find your state below to learn the specifics of their ink stamp and embosser requirements.

Alabama: Ink Stamp or Embossing seal required. All documents submitted for approval need the raised embossed seal.

Alaska: Ink Stamp or embossing seal required. Seal Impression must be photographable when using an embossing seal, it is necessary to use an impression inker with it.

Arizona: Ink Stamp required. Must use dark ink in the stamp (no color is specified by the Secretary of State). The embossing seal may only be used in addition to the ink stamp.

Arkansas: Ink Stamp or embossing seal required. Seal Impression must be photographable so when using an embossing seal, it is necessary to use an impression inker with it.

California: Ink Stamp or embossing seal required. Seal Impression must be photographable so when using an embossing seal, it is necessary to use an impression inker with it.

Colorado: Ink Stamp Required. It must contain the name of the notary, commission expiration date, the commission number, and the words "State of Colorado" and "Notary Public". Embossers are not allowed (after 2012).

Connecticut: Seal not required. Use of a seal is optional, state law does prescribe the format of the seal to be used.

Delaware: Ink Stamp or embossing seal required. Seal Impression must be photographable so when using an embossing seal, it is necessary to use an impression inker with it. Black ink is required in the use of the ink stamp.

District of Columbia: Embossing seal required. Seal impression must be photographable, so when using an embossing seal, it is necessary to use an impression inker with it. An ink stamp may be used, but only in addition to the embossing seal.

Florida: Ink Stamp required. The embossing seal may only be used in addition to the ink stamp.

Georgia: Ink Stamp or embossing seal required. Seal Impression must be photographable so when using an embossing seal, it is necessary to use an impression inker with it.

Hawaii: Ink stamp or embossing seal required.

Idaho: Ink Stamp required.

Illinois: Ink Stamp required. Black ink must be used.

Indiana: Ink Stamp or embossing seal required. Seal Impression must be photographable so when using an embossing seal, it is necessary to use an impression inker with it.

Iowa: Ink stamp or embossing seal required.

Kansas: Ink Stamp or embossing seal required. Seal Impression must be photographable so when using an embossing seal, it is necessary to use an impression inker with it.

Kentucky: Not required. It is optional but recommended.

Louisiana: Not required. It is optional but recommended.

Maine: Not required. It is optional but recommended.

Maryland: Ink Stamp or embossing seal required.

Massachusetts: Ink Stamp or embossing seal required. If you choose to use the ink stamp, black ink is required.

Michigan: Not required. It is optional but recommended. If you choose to use an official seal, the ink stamp may be used, but the embossing seal must be used in addition to the ink stamp

Minnesota: Ink Stamp required. Seal impression must be reproducible, so it is recommended when using an embossing seal to use an impression inker with it.

Mississippi: Ink Stamp required. Seal impression must be reproducibly, so it is recommended when using an embossing seal to use an impression inker with it.

Missouri: Ink Stamp or embossing seal required. If you choose to use the ink stamp, black ink is required.

Montana: Ink Stamp or embossing seal required. Blue or black ink is required. The stamp must be in the rectangular shape.

Nebraska: Ink Stamp or embossing seal required. Blue or black ink is required. The stamp must be in the rectangular shape.

Nevada: Ink stamp required. Seal impression must be photographically reproducible.

New Hampshire: Ink stamp or embossing seal required.

New Jersey: Not required. It is optional but recommended.

New Mexico: Ink stamp or embossing seal required.

New York: Not required. It is optional but recommended.

North Carolina. Ink stamp or embossing seal required. Seal impression must be photographically, so when using an embossing seal, it is necessary to use an impression inker with it.

North Dakota: Ink stamp required. Seal impression must be photographically.

Ohio: Ink stamp or embossing seal required.

Oklahoma: Ink stamp or embossing seal required.

Oregon: Ink stamp required. Black ink is required in the use of the ink stamp. An embossing seal may be used but only in addition to the ink stamp.

Pennsylvania: Ink Stamp required. The embossing seal may only be used in addition to the ink stamp.

Rhode Island: Not required. It is optional but recommended.

South Carolina: Ink Stamp or embossing seal strongly recommended. The absence of a notary seal or expiration date does not invalidate the notarial act only if the notary's official title is attached.

South Dakota: Ink stamp or embossing seal required

Tennessee: Ink Stamp required.

Texas: Ink Stamp or embossing seal required. Seal Impression must be photographically so when using an embossing seal, it is necessary to use an impression inker with it.

U.S Virgin Islands: Embossing seal required. An ink stamp may be used but only in addition to the embossing stamp.

Utah: Ink stamp required. An embossing seal may be used but only in addition to the ink stamp. The embossing seal must not be inked.

Vermont: Not required. Optional but recommended.

Virginia: Ink Stamp or embossing seal required. Seal Impression must be photographically so when using an embossing seal, it is necessary to use an impression inker with it.

Wisconsin: Ink stamp or embossing seal required.

West Virginia: Ink stamp required. An embossing seal may be used, but only in addition to the ink stamp.

Wyoming: Ink Stamp or embossing seal required. Seal Impression must be photographically so when using an embossing seal, it is necessary to use an impression inker with it.

> ***If a client asks you why you are or are not using a stamp or embosser, simply respond with your state's requirement for notarial acts. It would help to know exactly where to find that information in your state's notary handbook so you can show clients who are adamant about verification. ***

States also differ on whether notary journals are mandatory or simply recommended. It is good practice to keep a written record of the notarizations that you complete. Be sure to consult with your state's notary commissioning office to stay up to date on any changes on requirements.

States that require notary journals: Arizona, Arizona, California, Colorado, Delaware, District of Columbia, Hawaii, Illinois, Maryland, Massachusetts, Mississippi, Missouri, Montana, Nevada, Ohio, Oregon, Pennsylvania, Texas, Virginia (required only for electronic notarial acts.)

RECOMMENDATION: Keep a small bag/briefcase that holds all your notary supplies. Also keep an extra notary stamp/embosser in your vehicle so you will always be prepared to complete notarial acts.

PRINTERS FOR SIGNING AGENTS

It is crucial to your success as a signing agent, that you invest in a good quality dual tray laser printer. Each signing can have you printing anywhere from 50-250 pages! Any brand is fine, as long it is an all-in-one dual tray printer. I recommend the following printers that you can purchase from Amazon that would meet the basic standards suggested:

- Brother Business Color Laser Printer, HL-L8360CDWT, Wireless Networking, Automatic Duplex Printing, Mobile Printing, Cloud Printing, Amazon Dash Replenishment Enabled

  https://amzn.to/2OY6DUN

- HP LaserJet Pro M148dw All-in-One Wireless Monochrome Laser Printer with Auto Two-Sided Printing, Mobile Printing & Built-in Ethernet (4PA41A)

  https://amzn.to/2MTNMHL

- Brother Monochrome Laser Printer, HL-L6200DWT, Duplex Printing, Mobile Printing, Dual Paper Trays, Wireless Networking, Amazon Dash Replenishment Enabled

https://amzn.to/2J4NaxW

INSURANCE AND BONDS

Requirements for Errors & Omissions Insurance and Surety Bonds vary depending on what state you are commissioned in. Errors & Omissions insurance frequently referred to as E&O, is insurance that protects notaries themselves from liability. If an allegation/claim is made against an insured notary, the insurance provider will pay any legal fees/loss that the notary has been found responsible for up to the policy limits. Required/Recommended limits for E&O insurance vary by state as well.

Surety Bonds, usually just referred to as a bond, protect the signers in case of notary error, misconduct or fraudulent activity. This bond is a financial guarantee that the person who loses money will be reimbursed with up to the limits of said bond. It is important to note that the surety bond does not protect the notary as the E&O insurance does, which is why it is a good idea to have both, but at minimum if your state does not require bond be sure to have Errors & Omissions Insurance.

The National Notary Association (WWW.NATIONALNOTARY.ORG) helps notaries in all 50 states obtain Errors & Omissions Insurance and Surety

Bonds. This is a reputable organization that has been assisting notaries nationwide since 1957.

Bonds are currently required in each of the following states:

Alabama	Kansas	Oklahoma
Alaska	Kentucky	Pennsylvania
Arizona	Louisiana	South Dakota
Arkansas	Michigan	Tennessee
California	Mississippi	Texas
District of Columbia	Missouri	Utah
Florida	Montana	Washington
Hawaii	Nebraska	Wisconsin
Idaho	Nevada	Wyoming
Illinois	New Mexico	
Indiana	North Dakota	

A FEW MORE THINGS

Open a separate personal or business checking account as you will receive mostly checks from your real estate closings and would not want to frequent a check cashing establishment, as that will take away from your profit. It is recommended that notaries should get a bank account with mobile check deposit as it will allow you more control of your time as you can receive checks every day in your mailbox as your business grows. You do not need to open a business checking account if you will be conducting this business as a sole proprietor. If you are operating as a LLC, then you will need to open the business checking account. Some notaries do not LLC but you should weigh out the pros and cons to forming an LLC specific to your state and IRS tax reporting guidelines before making that decision.

You also want to design and order business cards. This will be an essential part to your marketing steps when acquiring local notary business. Your business cards should have your first and last name, phone number, business office address. (Home is optional but not advised. Keep in mind, using your home as your business address can result in people showing up at random times without calling ahead of time, looking for your notary services.) An address is not mandatory for your business card. Be sure to have a professional email. For instance, your name and then notary public at gmail.com is fine. (KrystalBanksnotarypublic@gmail.com) Keep it simple and professional. Also be sure to have your business card say Mobile Notary/Signing Agent.

Great! Now you are commissioned, insured and have all your supplies. It is time to start finding clients.

CHAPTER 3

<u>BECOMING A CERTIFIED SIGNING AGENT</u>

What is a loan signing agent?

Loan Signing Agents are notary publics who ensure proper execution of loan documents and are usually hired by escrow/title companies and signing service companies. It is their job to identify the signer(s) correctly, have them sign real estate loan documents and then notarize those documents.

As a signing agent, you will be contracted out by mortgage companies, title & escrow companies and signing companies. Signing service companies are entities that connect notaries/signing agents to clients (i.e title/mortgage companies) to complete loan closing appointments.

Whether contacted by a mortgage company, title/escrow company or a signing service, you will need to have your credentials prepared for easy submittal and review from said company. Simply create a folder on your desktop called "Notary Credentials". Be sure it includes a copy of your notary commission, Errors & Omission Insurance Declarations Page, Surety Bond Agreement, completed W-9, copy of your valid Driver's License and your E-Notary Credentials if applicable. This will make it simple and easy to submit this information to your requesting party and trust me, you will be submitting this a lot.

Another credential that most signing services and lenders want you to have is a certification from the National Notary Association (WWW.NATIONALNOTARY.ORG) called Signing Agent Certification. This credential is highly recommended but not required and you will take this every year to keep it current. The test is about 45 questions and open book.

The National Notary Association's certification program comes in three options (as pictured below). The basic package provides (1) background screening which most companies require you to have before you can conduct signing appointments with them, (2) the notary signing agent exam which is open book and covers basic loan document information, notary conduct and notary responsibilities during notarizations and (3) a 1-Year Listing on SigningAgent.com. The exam can be taken multiple times without any additional charge as well in case you do not obtain the necessary passing score on your first attempt.

Listings are important in helping to grow your business in that if a company is looking for a notary in your area, they can simply type in your zip code and your name along with others in your area will populate for them to choose from. It is also important to have a complete an accurate profile with a professional headshot photo to help your profile stand out from the additional notaries in your area. The other two packages provide additional training as a loan signing agent which is optional if you wish to take it prior to attending the Signing Agent Exam. You do not need to take their training to pass their test and obtain certification. There are books on Amazon written by different authors, including by the National Notary Association, that you can read in lieu of taking the online trainings.

Here is a link to one very popular training book from the National Notary Association found on Amazon:

Notary Signing Agent Certification Study Guide

https://amzn.to/2BaFgyJ

***You may also want to watch the videos on our YouTube channel at Notary2Notary as it will help give you more information about conducting loan closings.
https://www.youtube.com/channel/UChtRcuc0V8BfDKazh6mwcSQ ***

Choose Your Signing Agent Package

	BEST VALUE! **Complete NSA Certification** *Full Certification + Save 30% on Supplies* Order Now	**Basic NSA Certification** *Full Certification* Order Now	**NSA Background Screening Only** *Just the Minimum* Order Now
Background Screening Criminal background check; SSN required	✓	✓	✓
Continuing Education Exam	✓	✓	
1-Year SigningAgent.com Top-Tier Listing	✓	✓	
1-Year SigningAgent.com Priority Listing			✓
NSA Continuing Education Course	✓	✓	
Notary Essentials® Training	✓	✓	
The Notary Signing Agent's Loan Documents Sourcebook	✓		
Notary Signing Agent Invoices	✓		
Signing Agent Log	✓		
Notary Signing Agent Exam			✓
	$159 Order Now	**$99** Order Now	**$70** Order Now

It is highly recommended that you learn how to complete loan closings before you begin taking jobs to ensure the job is done correctly. If you make mistakes, like most commonly missing signatures, it can cause a client to not be able to refinance their home, lose their locked interest rate, cause a delay in funding and additional inconvenient delays. This will cause the company who hired you to not hire you for future jobs.

There are quite a few notary trainings available to you including the training provided by Notary2Notary, which includes training on how to pass the NNA Exam and feel confident as a Notary Signing Agent.

Visit www.notary2notary.com to register for an interactive program. This program includes an online course, forum, free webinars, access to knowledgeable notaries waiting to answer your questions, and updates within the notary industry.

Once you feel confident in your loan signing skills, you can begin accepting jobs from signing services and/or lenders. Typically, once contacted the hiring company will ask for your credentials, offer you a signing and then offer you a pay rate to complete this signing. You can accept the signing if you are available, decline the signing, or you can counter their pay offer BEFORE accepting the signing. If agreed upon, the company will then provide you with a notary confirmation via email which will spell out the appointment information as well as any additional requirements to complete the signing successfully.

The confirmation will also have the borrowers/client's information and when you should call them to confirm the appointment. Unless otherwise advised by the hiring company, you should always call a client before coming to their home.

The sky is the limit once you become a signing agent in that you can complete as many loan signings as you would like. After you complete your loan signing, you will be paid when and via the method agreed upon either in your signing confirmation or in the onboarding application you submitted to work with the hiring company.

Your confirmation is crucial to your closing appointment. Be sure to read it in its entirety because there may be necessary steps needed to complete this closing that may not be in your normal closing such as having a POA (power of attorney) or have the closing for a property located in an attorney state. These kinds of closings require a few additional steps to be completed accurately. Your confirmation is also going to confirm your agreed upon rate of pay. If you negotiated a higher rate, be sure before you complete that closing, that you have a new confirmation sent to you via email to protect your fee.

Below is what a typical confirmation page would look like:

TO:		**Scheduler:**		Order	
RE:		**Pages:**	5	Amrock/Quicken	
Base Fee:	$55.00	**Today's Date:**	8/26/2019	Loan #	
Email Fee:	$35.00	**Total Fee:**	$90.00	Appt Date: 8/30/2019	
2nd Loan Fee:	$0.00	**Your Deluxe eCheck will be sent:** 9/20/2019			

▶**Documents, when ready, will be posted on our website** https://www.jmtdocs.net/ **(just print 1 set)**

Fee Alert: You must report the status of the signing BEFORE leaving the signing. If you are still in the signing, and 60 minutes have elapsed, you must call JMT, ext 0, and report that you are still signing. Failure to do this WILL cause you to lose your fee.

UPON RECEIPT OF THIS ORDER CONFIRMATION

1. **PLEASE READ ALL INSTRUCTIONS ON THIS CONFIRMATION IMMEDIATELY.   FAILURE TO DO SO COULD CAUSE LOSS/REDUCTION OF YOUR FEE!**
2. Please go to https://www.jmtdocs.net/ to confirm that you have received this order. Should you fail to confirm receipt of this order, it may be assigned to another notary.
3. Cancellation requests are not official unless they come from JMT Documents Services!

BEFORE LEAVING THE SIGNING

1. Take time to review documents for complete accurate signatures, notary signature and seal.
2. You must go to https://www.jmtdocs.net/ or call JMT (0 for the operator) and report the status of the signing before you leave the signing. The status must be reported **WITHIN 60 MINUTES from the BEGINNING appointment time** (either by reporting on our website or calling our office). The lender requires this call. It is not negotiable.

AFTER THE SIGNING

Once the order has been marked "Signed", the order will be in "**Finalize Closing and Invoice**" status on our website https://www.jmtdocs.net/. Click on "Finalize Closing and Invoice" to submit an electronic invoice before 7:00 AM PST of the morning following the signing. The electronic invoice is all that is required; please do not submit self-made invoices.

RETURN THE DOCUMENTS

AMROCK 662 WOODWARD AVE, 10TH FLOOR DETROIT, MI 48226	**UPS #** SHIP THE DOCUMENTS THE SAME DAY IN THE OVERNIGHT ENVELOPE PROVIDED **Please drop the docs at a UPS store and get a receipt. If rural, a drop box may be used, but please list the name and location of the box below.**
UPS TRACKING #	Please enter your tracking number when asked, while submitting your electronic invoice on our website https://www.jmtdocs.net/

Submit invoice example (once you've marked the order 'Signed' you can click "Finalize closing and Invoice" to submit your electronic invoice)

Borrower	Address	City	Appt	Case #	Docs	Total Fee	Status	Action
TEST3	4150 S DEMAREE	VISALIA	07/11/2018	1005472	Online	$0	Signed	Finalize closing and Invoice

TITLE COMPANY:	Amrock / Quicken Loans
BORROWER:	▇▇▇▇▇▇ See #1 & 12 Below
CO-BORROWER:	▇▇▇▇ ▇▇
PHONE 1#	▇▇▇▇▇
SIGNING AT:	**Closing @ Panera Bread.**
	4701 Brad McNeer Pkwy., Midlothian, VA 23112
DATE and TIME:	**8/30/2019 at 09:00 AM**

SPECIAL INSTRUCTIONS: This is a Purchase Closing. You are meeting both the buyer and seller. Please check the closing instructions for fax/scan back requirements. (it is generally the 2nd or 3rd page of the docs you print out)

- Is This A Split Closing? - No

- Disbursement Date – 08/30/2019

- Who is Disbursing? – Amrock

- Who's Signing? –Buyer(s): ▇▇▇▇▇▇▇▇▇▇

- Seller(s): ▇▇▇▇▇▇▇▇

- Is the Seller Pre-Signing? – No

- Seller to Pay Current Water Bill? – No

- Did TSI Order a Final Water Bill?- No

- Who is Recording? – Amrock

- Are Docs Required to Record Before Disbursement? - Yes

- Seller Would Like Proceeds Via – Check via UPS Overnight

- Buyer/Agent Contact Info: ▇▇▇▇▇▇▇

- Seller/Agent Contact Info: ▇▇▇▇▇▇▇

AMROCK ADDITIONAL INSTRUCTIONS

1. To ensure the highest quality closing, please read all steps before asking the client (borrower) to begin signing. If you or the client has any questions, please contact Quicken Loans' Closing Hotline at 800-410-6799. If the client has questions or concerns, DO NOT leave the closing without making that call.

2. Follow any instructions on the "Notary closing instructions" included with the loan documents. You are not authorized to make changes or remove documents from the signing package. If you fail to abide by these instructions, you may suffer a financial loss.

3. **1003 Loan Application Form: If there is just one borrower, "NO SIGNATURE REQUIRED" will be typed on the signature line in the box located at the top of the 1003 Loan Application Form. The borrower will still need sign pages 3 and 4. If there are two borrowers both borrowers must sign pages 1, 3 & 4.**

4. Amrock, Quicken Loan, and Rock Financial do not require driver's license copies.

5. **Effective immediately:** If shipping UPS, please drop the signed package at The UPS Store, do NOT use the UPS Drop Box. And when dropping the package at the UPS Store, please obtain a receipt showing you dropped the package successfully.

   If you are unable to use the UPS Store, please notify Amrock that a drop box was used along with the time and the location the package was dropped.

   If you have any questions, please contact Amrock.

   Vendor Management Hotline: (888) 784-2514
   Signing Agent Services Team Hotline: (888) 784-2523

CHAPTER 4-
DETERMINING HOW TO CHARGE
FOR LOAN CLOSINGS VS STANDARD NOTARIZATIONS

When determining how much to charge to complete a loan closing, the rates can vary quite a bit. Charging for completing loan closings is very different than charging to complete standard day to day notarizations. For loan closings, the factors that should go into consideration are, time and location, number of pages you are required to print, number of signers and if fax/scan backs are required before shipping the documents. Faxbacks/scanbacks is the added step of scanning or faxing back the executed loan package back to the lender so they can review for any needed corrections or if needed for same-day funding.

It also depends, if the job is coming from a signing company or directly from the title/escrow company (Lender). We will go over the difference between the two in Chapter 5 (Signing Companies VS Escrow & Title Companies). A loan signing can pay anywhere from $50-$300 each. Since a loan closing can have anywhere from 1-30 notarizations, industry standard is to charge a standard lump sum fee that will cover all notarizations, time and travel.

This is the most disputed topic within the notary community, and I will not be able to tell you exactly what to accept or to charge as a definite answer, but I can provide a general guide.

We train notaries not to under charge for their services because this causes not only you to lose money but in turn hurts other notaries when companies begin to offer less money because there are notaries accepting a lesser fee than deserved.

When you are determining your rate for conducting standard notarizations, you must adhere to your state guidelines. Many states set limitations on what you are permitted to charge for notarizations and travel. It is important to stay within these parameters to prevent being in violation of your notary regulations, which can lead to commission revocation. For most, there is no clearly defined answer to what you can charge, and you will simply have to determine what your time and travel are worth as long as it is within the legalities of your state's regulations.

I would urge you to consider factors similar to a loan closing fee calculation: how far away are you traveling, how many pages, how many signers, is this a rush service or a holiday.

You can also call around to other notaries in your area and pretend to need their services and ask for quotes to get an idea of what notaries are charging in your area. You will see that there will be some really low quotes, super high quotes but most of them will in a general price point and you can use that to determine your prices. Remember this is your business, so you determine how it will be executed. You can also change your rates at any time if you determine that maybe your rates are too high or low.

There is so much that goes into your notary line of work that much of your learning will come in the field, as there will always be different types of documents or special requests that may be new to you.

In those cases, you can reach out to Notary2Notary (WWW.NOTARY2NOTARY.COM), check out notary forums/blogs and one of the best methods for quick answers I have found while in the field is a simple Google Search.

(Exception: If you have a question during a loan closing, ALWAYS call the hiring company or follow the hiring companies' instructions on who to call if you have questions. Making a mistake on a loan closing document is ONLY NOT your fault if you were incorrectly advised by the hiring company/lender.)

See chart below for State Maximum Fees:

State Maximum Fees For Common Notarial Acts				
State	**Acknowledgments**	**Jurats**	**Verbal Oath/Affirmation**	**Travel Fees/Other**
Alabama	$5	$5	$5	
Alaska	Notaries may set their fees			
Am. Samoa	$10 per signature	$10 per signature	$20 per person	
Arizona	$2 per signature	$2 per signature	$2 per person	
Arkansas	$5	$5	$5	
California	$10 per signature ($15 as of Jan. 1, 2017)	$10 per signature ($15 as of Jan. 1, 2017)	$10 per person ($15 as of Jan. 1, 2017)	
Colorado	$5 ($10 eNotarization)	$5 ($10 eNotarization)	$5	
Connecticut	$5	$5	$5	35 cents per mile
Delaware	$5 ($25 eNotarization)	$5 ($25 eNotarization)	$5	
DC	$5	$5	$5	
Florida	$10	$10	$10	Marriages: $30
Georgia	$2	$2	$2	
Guam	$10 first two signatures; $8 each additional signature	$10 first two signatures; $8 each additional signature	$10 per person	
Hawaii	$5 original + one duplicate, $2.50 for each duplicate after	$5 for original and four copies, $2.50 for each extra copy	$5 for original and four copies, $2.50 for each extra copy	
Idaho	$2	$2	$2	
Illinois	$1	$1	$1	$25 for documents related to residential real property transactions in Cook County
Indiana	$2	$2	$2	
Iowa	Notaries may set their fees			
Kansas	Notaries may set their fees			
Kentucky	Notaries may set their fees			
Louisiana	Notaries may set their fees			
Maine	Notaries may set their fees			
Maryland	$4	$4	$4	$5 plus 31 cents per mile
Massachusetts	Notaries may set their fees			
Michigan	$10	$10	$10	
Minnesota	$5	$5	$5	
Mississippi	$5	$5	$5	
Missouri	$2 per signature	$2 per signature	$1	
Virginia	$5 ($25 eNotarization)	$5 ($25 eNotarization)	$5	
Washington	$10	$10	$10	
West Virginia	$5 per signature	$5 per signature	$5	
Wisconsin	$5	$5	$5	
Wyoming	$5 per signature	$5 per signature	$5 per person	

CHAPTER 5

MARKETING YOUR NOTARY BUSINESS

The number one tip, I teach at Notary2Notary training is "Build your business through Marketing". The key to having your business grow by leaps and bounds is to have a great marketing strategy. According to Grant Cardone, the number one reason most businesses do not make sales is because of obscurity. No one can find you or the product or service you are selling.

Your brand/business must be able to be found online primarily. The number one way most successful notaries build their standard notarization business for local clientele is through Google. With a simple free website build and a free Google business page, you are set to begin receiving calls from your local audience.

Simple Website Build: You want to build a simple website using a free website building platform such as WEEBLY (www.weebly.com) or WIX

(www.wix.com) This website is going to allow you attract your day to day clients in your community who are looking for simple form notarizations. I suggest using one of their options to choose an already pre-built website where you are only adding basic text information to the website if you are not very tech-savvy.

YouTube has great videos to help navigate the Weebly platform as well.

Weebly Tutorial For Beginners 2019 | How To Build A Free Weebly Website
https://www.youtube.com/watch?v=f8Jgp45wu2s

We also have a Marketing 101 course at Notary2Notary as well to help you not only build your website but brand your business to attract more clients.

Your site should also have a Contact Us portion which allows visitors to contact you via email. You will usually receive emails that are asking if you can provide notary services and what specifically they will need done. You can simply respond with a follow up email asking for types of documents being notarized, number of pages, where will you be meeting them and what time they are available.

With this information, you should be able to provide them with an accurate quote and confirm their appointment time all via email. Be sure to ALWAYS ask for a contact phone number in case you are meeting somewhere that does not have a strong Wi-Fi connection.

As a notary, you can make a great deal of money from loan signings but that is not the only substantial way to make money in this industry. Additional potential clients include nursing facilities and hospice care agencies, hospitals, law firms, banks, political campaign groups and libraries. All of these companies and organizations will generally find you online, which is why the online presence is so important. However, to be proactive and increase your clientele, we suggest taking your business cards to these kinds of facilities in your area.

You want to simply let them know you are a mobile notary public and are local to the area so if they are ever in need of services, especially last-minute notarizations, you are available for same day appointments. We recommend taking at least one day a month to focus on card distribution to as many of these kinds of establishments as possible. Visiting the same establishment more than once is recommended if you have not heard from them within about a months' time.

***TIP: When you are leaving a facility or business after completing a notarization for someone who found you online, stop at the receptionist/front desk and simply say "Hi! My name is _____ and I am a mobile notary public. I visit this establishment doing notarizations for people here who find me online and I just wanted to leave some business cards if anyone comes to the front desk looking for a notary versus searching online." Be sure to smile and hand them the business cards. They almost always take the cards and more times than not they will call you when someone is need of a mobile notary.

MARKETING IS KEY!!!

Be sure when potential clients call, that you already have your rates pre-determined to allow you to provide a quick quote during the same call. You want to quote and book your client while on the phone to avoid losing their business because they WILL call another notary while they are waiting on you to give them a call back to provide your quote.

Another method of online advertisement is setting up a free Google Business Page. This page will allow people searching for mobile notaries in your area to not only see your location, hours and information about your business, but they can call or navigate directly to your office. 80% of my standard notarizations completed in the community are for people that who found me from my Google Business Page. In these days, we know that whenever we are looking for something, the first thing we do is "Hey Siri" or at least we do a simple Google Search. Make sure you are set up to be found by your local community.

*Send your Google Business page review link as a text message to all notary clients as soon as you finish notarizing their paperwork to increase your positive reviews. This will get your business page listed higher on Google when people are searching for a mobile notary.

CHAPTER 5
SIGNING COMPANIES VS ESCROW/TITLE COMPANIES

In the loan signing agent business, there are two general types of companies that will contract you to complete a loan signing appointment: Signing Services Companies or Escrow/Title Companies which for purposes of this chapter will be referred to as the Lender.

Signing Companies are businesses that serve as the middleman between a notary signing agent and the Lender. The signing company's main job is to locate qualified notaries who have experience in the loan signing industry and set up appointments for them to sign documents for the Lender's clients. The Lender pays the signing company a signing fee and from that fee the signing company pays a portion to the signing agent.

For example: Lender A has a couple who is **closing on a mortgage in two days and needs to find a qualified notary/signing agent to** conduct their closing since the Lender is in California and the couple is in Virginia. The Lender A calls a signing company called Signing Company B and tells them the couple wants to close on their loan in two days at 3pm at their home. The lender will provide the signing company B with the couple's closing documents as well as any additional information pertinent to their closing. They will then offer the signing company $250 to have the closing completed.

The signing company B will then contact signing agents in their own database to check for availability and if none exist, they will search else where like Notary Databases (i.e www.nationalnotary.org, www.123Notary.com, www.notaryrotary.com, www.notarycafe.com or Signingagent.com) and they also will simply Google notaries near the client's home address.

Once they can find a notary that is qualified, they will discuss the appointment and agree upon a fee that is to be paid to the notary upon successful completion of the signing. This is where negotiation becomes critical. Some signing companies are more than generous, some are decent and there are others who are downright wrong in what they are trying to offer you. You must remember that basically what ever you agree to accept, the balance is what the signing company can keep. (**You also should not ask the signing company how much they are being paid for the job.**)

Be sure to gather all the information about the appointment before agreeing to a fee such as location, time, estimated number of pages to be printed, scan/fax backs and whether you have to provide a witness. Providing a witness is not often expected of a signing agent but it does happen depending on the stipulations of the loan and what state the property is located in. If you are to provide a witness, you need to add that fee into the agreed upon fee which you will be responsible to paying directly to your witness.

Once a fee is agreed upon, the signing confirmation is sent to your email and you will have specific instructions to follow such as when to call the client and what to ask the client to provide. You will be sent documents that you may have to print to bring to the client's home to sign. There are times when the Lender will ship documents directly to the client. You will simply need to verify with the client before you arrive that they have in fact received the documents necessary to conduct the loan closing.

Upon successful completion of the signing, you scan/fax back copies of documents (if required) and then drop the documents in either a FEDEX or UPS box or shipping location. Once you have completed your signing, within 2-3 days you will know if you have made any errors that need to be corrected. If you did forget a signature, you will be required to go back out to the client's house to gather that signature at no additional payment to you. Therefore, is very important to take your time when going through the loan packages to ensure you do not miss any signatures.

Once the loan file is closed, you will be waiting to receive payment which can take anywhere from 2 weeks to 90 days depending on the signing companies' agreement. We do not recommend working for a company that pays out in 90 days as that is really an absurd time frame as signing companies are usually paid within a few days but up to 30 days at the latest for most transactions. For a company to hold that money for an extra 60 days is an inconvenience to you as a signing agent.

Now, when you receive closing appointments directly from the Lender (Escrow/Title Company) you are offered that higher fee usually between $150-$250 for each closing. The process is pretty much the same as far as receiving an email confirmation with instructions and loan documents to print.

You want to make good connections with the individual escrow officers to ensure that you are the first signing agent they call when they have closings available in your area. Basically, you would have to do two signings with a signing service to earn what you can potentially earn going directly to the source—The Lender.

There are advantages to starting with signing services in the beginning. The signing company will basically walk you through the process as they typically provide more than enough instruction pages to make sure you do not make any mistakes. Also, it is like you are working under a mask so to speak, in that if you make mistakes it is not really you that the Lender sees and remembers it is the signing company. However, if you go directly to the Lender and are fresh out of training and start making mistakes right out, they will most likely not use you again going forward. So, take the beginning months to practice and get it right with the signing companies so that way when you are ready to work with Lenders directly you impress them with your expertise.

At Notary2Notary, we conduct in-person trainings and online webinars to walk you through the signing process.

Ready to start working with signing companies?

Here is a list of our top recommended signing companies to get you started building your signing company database today:

1. SnapDocs https://www.snapdocs.com/
2. Amrock https://www.amrock.com/
3. Closing Exchange https://www.theclosingexchange.com/
4. JMT https://www.jmtdocs.net/SignerPortal/
5. Xpress Title https://www.xpresstitlellc.com/
6. X Marks The Spot http://xmssigningservices.com/
7. Signature Closers, LLC http://www.signatureclosers.com

You should also Google for additional signing companies, title companies and mortgage companies to connect with to increase your signing business.

**Be mindful in every industry there are companies that operate in poor business character. Stay updated with local forums and notary groups to find out what signing companies have poor reviews on how they treat and pay their signing agents. There have been quite a few who have been known to not pay notaries at all or until they are threaten with a lawsuit. Therefore, is very important to keep track of all your closings and notary appointments, the companies that hired you, the date you completed it and the agreed up on pay out date. You must keep track of this because the signing companies will not be as vigilant as you will be about receiving your payment. **

We recommend using NOTARY ASSIST to keep track of signings, companies you are working with and payments due to you. As your signings increase, you will need a system to help keep track of companies, orders and payments still pending/received. Companies pay anywhere from 2 weeks to 90 days so you will need a system in place to ensure you are paid correctly. There will be times when you will need to call companies to ask about payment that you have not received. It may have been an oversight, or it could have been sent to the wrong address that caused the delay. YOU NEED TO KEEP TRACK, because they will not keep track for you!

This software will also help you when it is time to file your year-end taxes. There is a $7.99 fee for this website monthly or $85 if paid annually. Visit

https://www.app.notaryassist.com/account/register#_a_N2N

NotaryAssist

CHAPTER 6-
HOW TO COMPLETE NOTARIZATIONS & SIGNINGS CORRECTLY

Completing notarizations correctly is crucial to not only gaining repeat clientele but to ensure you keep a clear notary record free from violations and claims.

Be sure to see valid identification for the signer in front of you before you have the client sign any documents. After you verify their identity, ALWAYS have the client sign the documents first - BEFORE you notarize the document.

Documents requiring notarizations are going to have varying notary section verbiage and the only way to make sure they are completed correctly is to read it. Read it out loud and make sense of what the document is saying.

The date is usually stated a bit different than what we typically read on everyday documents. It will typically say "Signed this _____day of _____,_____." This should be completed as follows: "Signed this 5th day of April 2019."

See examples:

STATE OF Virginia)

COUNTY OF Richmond) SS

Signer→ Timothy Jones
PRINT FULL NAME

Timothy Jones
SIGNATURE

Sworn to and subscribed before me this 23rd day of March , 20 18 .

Krystal Banks
Notary Public

Notary Seal = Stamp Here

SELLER(S):

Brian Jackson
Seller 1 Name

Lisa Jackson
Seller 2 Name

> A notary public or other officer completing this certificate verifies only the identity of the individual who signed the document, to which this certificate is attached, and not the truthfulness, accuracy, or validity of that document.

State of California

County of _Alameda_

On, _March 2, 2019_ before me _Krystal Banks, Notary Public_
(Shown name and capacity)

Personally appeared _Brian Jackson and Lisa Jackson_,
(or proved to me on the basis of satisfactory evidence) to be the person(s), whose name(s) is/are subscribed to the within instrument and acknowledged to be that he/she/they executed the same in his/her/their authorized capacity(ies), and that by his/her/their signature(s) on the instrument the person(s) or the entity upon behalf of which the person(s) acted, executed the instrument.

WITNESS my hand and official seal,

Signature: _Krystal Banks_   → Stamp Here ←

(This area for official notarial seal)

When completing loan closings, you should familiarize yourself with a few of the consistently present documents such as the closing disclosure, the deed, the note and the signature name affidavit.

Closing Disclosure - The Closing Disclosure is a five-page document that provides final figures for a mortgage. It includes the loan terms, estimated monthly payments, and how much will be paid in fees and closing costs. This document also has the contact information for both the loan officer and the title/settlement company. The lender is required to give the borrower the Closing Disclosure at least three business days before you close on the mortgage loan. This three-day window allows time to review final terms and costs before the borrower meets with you at the closing table. The closing disclosure will also have at the bottom of the first page a section called CASH TO CLOSE. This section will have an amount and beside it will either be checked: **From borrower or To borrower. This is very important!** If the box is checked to borrower, you simply let the borrower know this is the amount they will receive back once the transaction has fully closed. There will usually be a form in the package for the borrower to complete asking how they would like to receive those funds (check or wire). If the box is checked that says from borrower, then that is the amount that the borrower needs to pay at closing/on closing day. Sometimes the borrower will tell you that they have already sent the wire in and at that point you simply let the hiring company/Lender know that the borrower has advised they have already submitted the funds required to close. This can be done by a simple email at the table. The borrower may also have a personal check/cashier check for you at the table. You want to be sure you check your state law as some states prohibit notaries from handling the money transfer portion of real estate transactions. If you are in one of those states, then usually the Lender will provide an extra shipping label for you to give the client for them to mail the check themselves. If the borrower says they were not aware of the closing costs due and are not prepared to pay them, you must stop the closing and call the loan officer immediately. They will advise you on how they wish to proceed.

See sample Closing Disclosure:

Closing Disclosure

This form is a statement of final loan terms and closing costs. Compare this document with your Loan Estimate.

Closing Information

Date Issued	4/15/2013
Closing Date	4/15/2013
Disbursement Date	4/15/2013
Settlement Agent	Epsilon Title Co.
File #	12-3456
Property	456 Somewhere Ave
	Anytown, ST 12345
Sale Price	$180,000

Transaction Information

Borrower	Michael Jones and Mary Stone
	123 Anywhere Street
	Anytown, ST 12345
Seller	Steve Cole and Amy Doe
	321 Somewhere Drive
	Anytown, ST 12345
Lender	Ficus Bank

Loan Information

Loan Term	30 years
Purpose	Purchase
Product	Fixed Rate
Loan Type	☒ Conventional ☐ FHA
	☐ VA ☐ _____
Loan ID #	123456789
MIC #	000654321

Loan Terms

		Can this amount increase after closing?
Loan Amount	$162,000	NO
Interest Rate	3.875%	NO
Monthly Principal & Interest *See Projected Payments below for your Estimated Total Monthly Payment*	$761.78	NO
		Does the loan have these features?
Prepayment Penalty		YES • As high as **$3,240** if you pay off the loan during the first 2 years
Balloon Payment		NO

Projected Payments

Payment Calculation	Years 1-7	Years 8-30
Principal & Interest	$761.78	$761.78
Mortgage Insurance	+ 82.35	+ —
Estimated Escrow *Amount can increase over time*	+ 206.13	+ 206.13
Estimated Total Monthly Payment	**$1,050.26**	**$967.91**

Estimated Taxes, Insurance & Assessments *Amount can increase over time* *See page 4 for details*	$356.13 a month	**This estimate includes** ☒ Property Taxes ☒ Homeowner's Insurance ☒ Other: Homeowner's Association Dues *See Escrow Account on page 4 for details. You must pay for other property costs separately.*	**In escrow?** YES YES NO

Costs at Closing

Closing Costs	$9,712.10	Includes $4,694.05 in Loan Costs + $5,018.05 in Other Costs – $0 in Lender Credits. *See page 2 for details.*
Cash to Close	$14,147.26	Includes Closing Costs. *See Calculating Cash to Close on page 3 for details.*

Closing Cost Details

Loan Costs		Borrower-Paid		Seller-Paid		Paid by Others
		At Closing	Before Closing	At Closing	Before Closing	
A. Origination Charges		**$1,802.00**				
01 0.25 % of Loan Amount (Points)		$405.00				
02 Application Fee		$300.00				
03 Underwriting Fee		$1,097.00				
04						
05						
06						
07						
08						
B. Services Borrower Did Not Shop For		**$236.55**				
01 Appraisal Fee	to John Smith Appraisers Inc.					$405.00
02 Credit Report Fee	to Information Inc.		$29.80			
03 Flood Determination Fee	to Info Co.	$20.00				
04 Flood Monitoring Fee	to Info Co.	$31.75				
05 Tax Monitoring Fee	to Info Co.	$75.00				
06 Tax Status Research Fee	to Info Co.	$80.00				
07						
08						
09						
10						
C. Services Borrower Did Shop For		**$2,655.50**				
01 Pest Inspection Fee	to Pests Co.	$120.50				
02 Survey Fee	to Surveys Co.	$85.00				
03 Title – Insurance Binder	to Epsilon Title Co.	$650.00				
04 Title – Lender's Title Insurance	to Epsilon Title Co.	$500.00				
05 Title – Settlement Agent Fee	to Epsilon Title Co.	$500.00				
06 Title – Title Search	to Epsilon Title Co.	$800.00				
07						
08						
D. TOTAL LOAN COSTS (Borrower-Paid)		**$4,694.05**				
Loan Costs Subtotals (A + B + C)		$4,664.25	$29.80			

Other Costs						
E. Taxes and Other Government Fees		**$85.00**				
01 Recording Fees	Deed: $40.00 Mortgage: $45.00	$85.00				
02 Transfer Tax	to Any State			$950.00		
F. Prepaids		**$2,120.80**				
01 Homeowner's Insurance Premium (12 mo.) to Insurance Co.		$1,209.96				
02 Mortgage Insurance Premium (mo.)						
03 Prepaid Interest ($17.44 per day from 4/15/13 to 5/1/13)		$279.04				
04 Property Taxes (6 mo.) to Any County USA		$631.80				
05						
G. Initial Escrow Payment at Closing		**$412.25**				
01 Homeowner's Insurance $100.83 per month for 2 mo.		$201.66				
02 Mortgage Insurance per month for mo.						
03 Property Taxes $105.30 per month for 2 mo.		$210.60				
04						
05						
06						
07						
08 Aggregate Adjustment		– 0.01				
H. Other		**$2,400.00**				
01 HOA Capital Contribution	to HOA Acre Inc.	$500.00				
02 HOA Processing Fee	to HOA Acre Inc.	$150.00				
03 Home Inspection Fee	to Engineers Inc.	$750.00			$750.00	
04 Home Warranty Fee	to XYZ Warranty Inc.			$450.00		
05 Real Estate Commission	to Alpha Real Estate Broker			$5,700.00		
06 Real Estate Commission	to Omega Real Estate Broker			$5,700.00		
07 Title – Owner's Title Insurance (optional) to Epsilon Title Co.		$1,000.00				
08						
I. TOTAL OTHER COSTS (Borrower-Paid)		**$5,018.05**				
Other Costs Subtotals (E + F + G + H)		$5,018.05				

J. TOTAL CLOSING COSTS (Borrower-Paid)		**$9,712.10**				
Closing Costs Subtotals (D + I)		$9,682.30	$29.80	$12,800.00	$750.00	$405.00
Lender Credits						

Calculating Cash to Close

Use this table to see what has changed from your Loan Estimate.

	Loan Estimate	Final	Did this change?
Total Closing Costs (J)	$8,054.00	$9,712.10	YES • See **Total Loan Costs (D)** and **Total Other Costs (I)**
Closing Costs Paid Before Closing	$0	– $29.80	YES • You paid these Closing Costs **before closing**
Closing Costs Financed (Paid from your Loan Amount)	$0	$0	NO
Down Payment/Funds from Borrower	$18,000.00	$18,000.00	NO
Deposit	– $10,000.00	– $10,000.00	NO
Funds for Borrower	$0	$0	NO
Seller Credits	$0	– $2,500.00	YES • See Seller Credits in **Section L**
Adjustments and Other Credits	$0	– $1,035.04	YES • See details in **Sections K and L**
Cash to Close	$16,054.00	$14,147.26	

Summaries of Transactions

Use this table to see a summary of your transaction.

BORROWER'S TRANSACTION

K. Due from Borrower at Closing		$189,762.30
01 Sale Price of Property		$180,000.00
02 Sale Price of Any Personal Property Included in Sale		
03 Closing Costs Paid at Closing (J)		$9,682.30
04		
Adjustments		
05		
06		
07		
Adjustments for Items Paid by Seller in Advance		
08 City/Town Taxes	to	
09 County Taxes	to	
10 Assessments	to	
11 HOA Dues	4/15/13 to 4/30/13	$80.00
12		
13		
14		
15		

L. Paid Already by or on Behalf of Borrower at Closing		$175,615.04
01 Deposit		$10,000.00
02 Loan Amount		$162,000.00
03 Existing Loan(s) Assumed or Taken Subject to		
04		
05 Seller Credit		$2,500.00
Other Credits		
06 Rebate from Epsilon Title Co.		$750.00
07		
Adjustments		
08		
09		
10		
11		
Adjustments for Items Unpaid by Seller		
12 City/Town Taxes	1/1/13 to 4/14/13	$365.04
13 County Taxes	to	
14 Assessments	to	
15		
16		
17		

SELLER'S TRANSACTION

M. Due to Seller at Closing		$180,080.00
01 Sale Price of Property		$180,000.00
02 Sale Price of Any Personal Property Included in Sale		
03		
04		
05		
06		
07		
08		
Adjustments for Items Paid by Seller in Advance		
09 City/Town Taxes	to	
10 County Taxes	to	
11 Assessments	to	
12 HOA Dues	4/15/13 to 4/30/13	$80.00
13		
14		
15		
16		

N. Due from Seller at Closing		$115,665.04
01 Excess Deposit		
02 Closing Costs Paid at Closing (J)		$12,800.00
03 Existing Loan(s) Assumed or Taken Subject to		
04 Payoff of First Mortgage Loan		$100,000.00
05 Payoff of Second Mortgage Loan		
06		
07		
08 Seller Credit		$2,500.00
09		
10		
11		
12		
13		
Adjustments for Items Unpaid by Seller		
14 City/Town Taxes	1/1/13 to 4/14/13	$365.04
15 County Taxes	to	
16 Assessments	to	
17		
18		
19		

CALCULATION

Total Due from Borrower at Closing (K)	$189,762.30
Total Paid Already by or on Behalf of Borrower at Closing (L)	– $175,615.04
Cash to Close ☒ From ☐ To Borrower	**$14,147.26**

CALCULATION

Total Due to Seller at Closing (M)	$180,080.00
Total Due from Seller at Closing (N)	– $115,665.04
Cash ☐ From ☒ To Seller	**$64,414.96**

Additional Information About This Loan

Loan Disclosures

Assumption
If you sell or transfer this property to another person, your lender
- [ ] will allow, under certain conditions, this person to assume this loan on the original terms.
- [X] will not allow assumption of this loan on the original terms.

Demand Feature
Your loan
- [ ] has a demand feature, which permits your lender to require early repayment of the loan. You should review your note for details.
- [X] does not have a demand feature.

Late Payment
If your payment is more than *15* days late, your lender will charge a late fee of *5% of the monthly principal and interest payment.*

Negative Amortization (Increase in Loan Amount)
Under your loan terms, you
- [ ] are scheduled to make monthly payments that do not pay all of the interest due that month. As a result, your loan amount will increase (negatively amortize), and your loan amount will likely become larger than your original loan amount. Increases in your loan amount lower the equity you have in this property.
- [ ] may have monthly payments that do not pay all of the interest due that month. If you do, your loan amount will increase (negatively amortize), and, as a result, your loan amount may become larger than your original loan amount. Increases in your loan amount lower the equity you have in this property.
- [X] do not have a negative amortization feature.

Partial Payments
Your lender
- [X] may accept payments that are less than the full amount due (partial payments) and apply them to your loan.
- [ ] may hold them in a separate account until you pay the rest of the payment, and then apply the full payment to your loan.
- [ ] does not accept any partial payments.
If this loan is sold, your new lender may have a different policy.

Security Interest
You are granting a security interest in
456 Somewhere Ave., Anytown, ST 12345

You may lose this property if you do not make your payments or satisfy other obligations for this loan.

Escrow Account
For now, your loan
- [X] will have an escrow account (also called an "impound" or "trust" account) to pay the property costs listed below. Without an escrow account, you would pay them directly, possibly in one or two large payments a year. Your lender may be liable for penalties and interest for failing to make a payment.

Escrow		
Escrowed Property Costs over Year 1	$2,473.56	Estimated total amount over year 1 for your escrowed property costs: *Homeowner's Insurance Property Taxes*
Non-Escrowed Property Costs over Year 1	$1,800.00	Estimated total amount over year 1 for your non-escrowed property costs: *Homeowner's Association Dues* You may have other property costs.
Initial Escrow Payment	$412.25	A cushion for the escrow account you pay at closing. See Section G on page 2.
Monthly Escrow Payment	$206.13	The amount included in your total monthly payment.

- [ ] will not have an escrow account because [ ] you declined it [ ] your lender does not offer one. You must directly pay your property costs, such as taxes and homeowner's insurance. Contact your lender to ask if your loan can have an escrow account.

No Escrow		
Estimated Property Costs over Year 1		Estimated total amount over year 1. You must pay these costs directly, possibly in one or two large payments a year.
Escrow Waiver Fee		

In the future,
Your property costs may change and, as a result, your escrow payment may change. You may be able to cancel your escrow account, but if you do, you must pay your property costs directly. If you fail to pay your property taxes, your state or local government may (1) impose fines and penalties or (2) place a tax lien on this property. If you fail to pay any of your property costs, your lender may (1) add the amounts to your loan balance, (2) add an escrow account to your loan, or (3) require you to pay for property insurance that the lender buys on your behalf, which likely would cost more and provide fewer benefits than what you could buy on your own.

Loan Calculations

Total of Payments. Total you will have paid after you make all payments of principal, interest, mortgage insurance, and loan costs, as scheduled.	$285,803.36
Finance Charge. The dollar amount the loan will cost you.	$118,830.27
Amount Financed. The loan amount available after paying your upfront finance charge.	$162,000.00
Annual Percentage Rate (APR). Your costs over the loan term expressed as a rate. This is not your interest rate.	4.174%
Total Interest Percentage (TIP). The total amount of interest that you will pay over the loan term as a percentage of your loan amount.	69.46%

 Questions? If you have questions about the loan terms or costs on this form, use the contact information below. To get more information or make a complaint, contact the Consumer Financial Protection Bureau at **www.consumerfinance.gov/mortgage-closing**

Other Disclosures

Appraisal
If the property was appraised for your loan, your lender is required to give you a copy at no additional cost at least 3 days before closing. If you have not yet received it, please contact your lender at the information listed below.

Contract Details
See your note and security instrument for information about
- what happens if you fail to make your payments,
- what is a default on the loan,
- situations in which your lender can require early repayment of the loan, and
- the rules for making payments before they are due.

Liability after Foreclosure
If your lender forecloses on this property and the foreclosure does not cover the amount of unpaid balance on this loan,

☒ state law may protect you from liability for the unpaid balance. If you refinance or take on any additional debt on this property, you may lose this protection and have to pay any debt remaining even after foreclosure. You may want to consult a lawyer for more information.

☐ state law does not protect you from liability for the unpaid balance.

Refinance
Refinancing this loan will depend on your future financial situation, the property value, and market conditions. You may not be able to refinance this loan.

Tax Deductions
If you borrow more than this property is worth, the interest on the loan amount above this property's fair market value is not deductible from your federal income taxes. You should consult a tax advisor for more information.

Contact Information

	Lender	Mortgage Broker	Real Estate Broker (B)	Real Estate Broker (S)	Settlement Agent
Name	Ficus Bank		Omega Real Estate Broker Inc.	Alpha Real Estate Broker Co.	Epsilon Title Co.
Address	4321 Random Blvd. Somecity, ST 12340		789 Local Lane Sometown, ST 12345	987 Suburb Ct. Someplace, ST 12340	123 Commerce Pl. Somecity, ST 12344
NMLS ID					
ST License ID			Z765416	Z61456	Z61616
Contact	Joe Smith		Samuel Green	Joseph Cain	Sarah Arnold
Contact NMLS ID	12345				
Contact ST License ID			P16415	P51461	PT1234
Email	joesmith@ ficusbank.com		sam@omegare.biz	joe@alphare.biz	sarah@ epsilontitle.com
Phone	123-456-7890		123-555-1717	321-555-7171	987-555-4321

Confirm Receipt

By signing, you are only confirming that you have received this form. You do not have to accept this loan because you have signed or received this form.

_____ _____
Applicant Signature   Date

_____ _____
Co-Applicant Signature   Date

Deed of Trust- This document is basically an agreement between a lender and a borrower to transfer an interest in the borrower's land to a neutral third party, a trustee, to secure the payment of a debt by the borrower. In exchange for a loan of money from the lender, the borrower places legal title to real property in the hands of the trustee who holds it for the benefit of the lender, named in the deed as the beneficiary. The borrower retains equitable title to, and possession of, the property.

For the purposes of loan signing, you simply need to point out who is on the deed. Usually, it is the borrower and possibly a non-borrowing spouse, or there may be two borrowers and they are both on the deed. Anyone can be put on the deed of the property; however, your only job is pointing out who is on it. If the deed is wrong, you will need to stop the signing and immediately call the loan officer.

See example:

After Recording Return To:

_____
_____
_____
_____

_____ **[Space Above This Line For Recording Data]** _____

DEED OF TRUST

DEFINITIONS

Words used in multiple sections of this document are defined below and other words are defined in Sections 3, 11, 13, 18, 20 and 21. Certain rules regarding the usage of words used in this document are also provided in Section 16.

(A) "Security Instrument" means this document, which is dated _____ , _____ , together with all Riders to this document.
(B) "Borrower" is _____ . Borrower is the trustor under this Security Instrument.
(C) "Lender" is _____ . Lender is a _____ organized and existing under the laws of _____ _____ . Lender's address is _____ _____ . Lender is the beneficiary under this Security Instrument.
(D) "Trustee" is _____ .
(E) "Note" means the promissory note signed by Borrower and dated _____ , _____ . The Note states that Borrower owes Lender _____ Dollars (U.S. $_____) plus interest. Borrower has promised to pay this debt in regular Periodic Payments and to pay the debt in full not later than _____ .
(F) "Property" means the property that is described below under the heading "Transfer of Rights in the Property."
(G) "Loan" means the debt evidenced by the Note, plus interest, any prepayment charges and late charges due under the Note, and all sums due under this Security Instrument, plus interest.
(H) "Riders" means all Riders to this Security Instrument that are executed by Borrower. The following Riders are to be executed by Borrower [check box as applicable]:

☐ Adjustable Rate Rider ☐ Condominium Rider ☐ Second Home Rider
☐ Balloon Rider ☐ Planned Unit Development Rider ☐ Other(s) [specify]_____
☐ 1-4 Family Rider ☐ Biweekly Payment Rider

Note- The note is a document that an individual signs with a lender by pledging the property against the money that is borrowed. On this document the main things you should point out is when the client's first payment due and how many days they have make their payment before a late fee is applied.

*Remember the monthly payment listed on the Note, is NOT the estimated monthly payment they will be paying each month as it does not include the property taxes and homeowner's insurance and any other items they pay monthly within their monthly payment if applicable. Advise them the final estimated monthly payment is on the Closing Disclosure. ***

See Example:

NOTE

_____, ___   _____, ___   _____
[Date]   [City]   [State]

_____
[Property Address]

1. BORROWER'S PROMISE TO PAY

In return for a loan that I have received, I promise to pay U.S. $_____ (this amount is called "Principal"), plus interest, to the order of the Lender. The Lender is _____. I will make all payments under this Note in the form of cash, check or money order.

I understand that the Lender may transfer this Note. The Lender or anyone who takes this Note by transfer and who is entitled to receive payments under this Note is called the "Note Holder."

2. INTEREST

Interest will be charged on unpaid principal until the full amount of Principal has been paid. I will pay interest at a yearly rate of _____%.

The interest rate required by this Section 2 is the rate I will pay both before and after any default described in Section 6(B) of this Note.

3. PAYMENTS

(A) Time and Place of Payments

I will pay principal and interest by making a payment every month.

I will make my monthly payment on the _____ day of each month beginning on _____, ____. I will make these payments every month until I have paid all of the principal and interest and any other charges described below that I may owe under this Note. Each monthly payment will be applied as of its scheduled due date and will be applied to interest before Principal. If, on _____, 20___, I still owe amounts under this Note, I will pay those amounts in full on that date, which is called the "Maturity Date."

I will make my monthly payments at _____ or at a different place if required by the Note Holder.

(B) Amount of Monthly Payments

My monthly payment will be in the amount of U.S. $_____.

4. BORROWER'S RIGHT TO PREPAY

I have the right to make payments of Principal at any time before they are due. A payment of Principal only is known as a "Prepayment." When I make a Prepayment, I will tell the Note Holder in writing that I am doing so. I may not designate a payment as a Prepayment if I have not made all the monthly payments due under the Note.

I may make a full Prepayment or partial Prepayments without paying a Prepayment charge. The Note Holder will use my Prepayments to reduce the amount of Principal that I owe under this Note. However, the Note Holder may apply my Prepayment to the accrued and unpaid interest on the Prepayment amount, before applying my Prepayment to reduce the Principal amount of the Note. If I make a partial Prepayment, there will be no changes in the due date or in the amount of my monthly payment unless the Note Holder agrees in writing to those changes.

5. LOAN CHARGES

If a law, which applies to this loan and which sets maximum loan charges, is finally interpreted so that the interest or other loan charges collected or to be collected in connection with this loan exceed the permitted limits, then: (a) any such loan charge shall be reduced by the amount necessary to reduce the charge to the permitted limit; and (b) any sums already collected from me which exceeded permitted limits will be refunded to me. The Note Holder may choose to make this refund by reducing the Principal I owe under this Note or by making a direct payment to me. If a refund reduces Principal, the reduction will be treated as a partial Prepayment.

6. BORROWER'S FAILURE TO PAY AS REQUIRED

(A) Late Charge for Overdue Payments

If the Note Holder has not received the full amount of any monthly payment by the end of _____ calendar days after the date it is due, I will pay a late charge to the Note Holder. The amount of the charge will be ____% of my overdue payment of principal and interest. I will pay this late charge promptly but only once on each late payment.

(B) Default

If I do not pay the full amount of each monthly payment on the date it is due, I will be in default.

(C) Notice of Default

If I am in default, the Note Holder may send me a written notice telling me that if I do not pay the overdue amount by a certain date, the Note Holder may require me to pay immediately the full amount of Principal which has not been paid and all the interest that I owe on that amount. That date must be at least 30 days after the date on which the notice is mailed to me or delivered by other means.

(D) No Waiver By Note Holder

Even if, at a time when I am in default, the Note Holder does not require me to pay immediately in full as described above, the Note Holder will still have the right to do so if I am in default at a later time.

(E) Payment of Note Holder's Costs and Expenses

If the Note Holder has required me to pay immediately in full as described above, the Note Holder will have the right to be paid back by me for all of its costs and expenses in enforcing this Note to the extent not prohibited by applicable law. Those expenses include, for example, reasonable attorneys' fees.

7. GIVING OF NOTICES

Unless applicable law requires a different method, any notice that must be given to me under this Note will be given by delivering it or by mailing it by first class mail to me at the Property Address above or at a different address if I give the Note Holder a notice of my different address.

Any notice that must be given to the Note Holder under this Note will be given by delivering it or by mailing it by first class mail to the Note Holder at the address stated in Section 3(A) above or at a different address if I am given a notice of that different address.

8. OBLIGATIONS OF PERSONS UNDER THIS NOTE

If more than one person signs this Note, each person is fully and personally obligated to keep all of the promises made in this Note, including the promise to pay the full amount owed. Any person who is a guarantor, surety or endorser of this Note is also obligated to do these things. Any person who takes over these obligations, including the obligations of a guarantor, surety or endorser of this Note, is also obligated to keep all of the promises made in this Note. The Note Holder may enforce its rights under this Note against each person individually or against all of us together. This means that any one of us may be required to pay all of the amounts owed under this Note.

9. WAIVERS

I and any other person who has obligations under this Note waive the rights of Presentment and Notice of Dishonor and waive the benefit of the homestead exemption as to the Property described in the Security Instrument (as defined below). "Presentment" means the right to require the Note Holder to demand payment of amounts due. "Notice of Dishonor" means the right to require the Note Holder to give notice to other persons that amounts due have not been paid.

10. UNIFORM SECURED NOTE

This Note is a uniform instrument with limited variations in some jurisdictions. In addition to the protections given to the Note Holder under this Note, a Mortgage, Deed of Trust, or Security Deed (the "Security Instrument"), dated the same date as this Note, protects the Note Holder from possible losses which might result if I do not keep the promises which I make in this Note. That Security Instrument describes how and under what conditions I may be required to make immediate payment in full of all amounts I owe under this Note. Some of those conditions are described as follows:

If all or any part of the Property or any Interest in the Property is sold or transferred (or if Borrower is not a natural person and a beneficial interest in Borrower is sold or transferred) without Lender's prior written consent, Lender may require immediate payment in full of all sums secured by this Security Instrument. However, this option shall not be exercised by Lender if such exercise is prohibited by Applicable Law.

If Lender exercises this option, Lender shall give Borrower notice of acceleration. The notice shall provide a period of not less than 30 days from the date the notice is given in accordance with Section 15 within which Borrower must pay all sums secured by this Security Instrument. If Borrower fails to pay these sums prior to the expiration of this period, Lender may invoke any remedies permitted by this Security Instrument without further notice or demand on Borrower.

WITNESS THE HAND(S) AND SEAL(S) OF THE UNDERSIGNED.

_____ (Seal)
                                -Borrower

_____ (Seal)
                                -Borrower

_____ (Seal)
                                -Borrower

[Sign Original Only]

Signature Name Affidavit-A signature name affidavit is a document in which the signatory affirms that his or her legal name is written and typed as stated in the affidavit.

The affidavit can have just one name or several for the client to affirm that they are also their legal/former legal names. This is most frequent with maiden names and person's with suffixes like Jr and IV. They need to sign each name if it is or has been their name before. If it is completely wrong and has never been their name, then you would simply have them write "NEVER BEEN KNOW AS" and then initial it.

See example:

SIGNATURE/NAME AFFIDAVIT AND AKA STATEMENT

DATE: 08/03/1990   FILE NO.: _054648694_

BORROWER: _____ Ricardo Jennings _____

THIS IS TO CERTIFY THAT MY LEGAL SIGNATURE IS AS WRITTEN AND TYPED BELOW.
(This signature must <u>exactly</u> match signatures on all Closing Documents.)

_____ Ricardo Jennings _____   _Ricardo Jinnys_
(Print or Type Name)   Signature

AKA STATEMENT

I, _____ Ricardo Jennings _____   certify that I am also known as:

_____ Ricardo B Jennings _____   _Ricondu B Jinyp_
Print Name (Variation)   Sample Signature (Variation)

_____   _____
Print Name (Variation)   Sample Signature (Variation)

_____   _____
Print Name (Variation)   Sample Signature (Variation)

STATE OF VIRGINIA   )
) ss
COUNTY OF CHESTERFIELD   )

Subscribed and sworn to before me this 12ᵗʰ day of April _____, 20 19 , by
Ricardo Jennings _____ , personally known to me or proved to me on
the basis of satisfactory evidence to be the person who appeared before me.

Krystul Bants
Notary Public   Stamp Here

These 5 documents are in almost every closing you will do, so take the time and get familiar with them so when the borrower has questions you can answer then intelligently without needing to call the loan officer or hiring company several times in one closing. This not only lets the hiring company know that you are inexperienced, but it extends your time at the client's house.

Experienced and properly trained notaries can complete a closing within 15-30 minutes. A reverse mortgage closing which usually has twice the paperwork can take between 30-60 minutes. You want to be efficient in your time so you can accommodate more signings in your schedule.

TOP 3 THINGS TO REMEMBER

1. READ, READ, READ! Read you email confirmation to make sure you follow the stipulations required to close this transaction and not waste your time doing it wrong.

2. DOUBLE CHECK! Even the best signing agents can miss signatures if they do not double check their work. At the table, you may end up having a great conversation with the client and get distracted. It happens. Once you have finished the package take an extra 2-5 minutes and review the package for missed signatures. It is better to do this now than to submit the package wrong and have to drive back out to the client's house and collect the signatures again.

3. DROP THE PACKAGES ON TIME!! Same day drops are expected however depending on the time of the closing it may permitted to drop the next day. You must make that drop by the next day or the client's loan can be delayed which will make not only make the client unhappy but also the Lender.

CHAPTER 7-

EXPERIENCE IS THE BEST TEACHER

As a mobile notary public/loan signing agent, you are going to be meeting all kinds of people and often in their homes! This chapter is very important because it prepares you for what you may not have expected. When you are going into different people's homes several times a day, five/six days a week, you will meet a variety of different people in different spaces that you will be required to adjust to. Let's review the big three and the best way to handle these situations.

Big One: PETS!

The number one thing you will have to deal with, as a mobile signing agent is the pets in signer's homes. Sometimes the clients will put their dogs/cats up for you as a courtesy but do not expect that. There are times when clients can be offended if you have an issue with their animal as some people view them as equals in the household. You need to be able to contain your composure and complete the signing, if your safety is not in danger. Sometimes dogs will jump on you and lick you and the client may try to restrain them. However, there are clients who do not see anything wrong with that.

I have had two clients have their cats walk back and forth across the table and paperwork with a weak attempt of shooing them away for them to simply return. I have had groups of dogs surround my chair at a signing sniffing and barking and jumping on my lap. Of course, you can absolutely ask for the owners to restrain their animals if they are physically touching you as at that point, they have gone a bit too far.

The best way to handle pets is to be pleasant and remain calm. Simply focus on completing the signing as quickly and ACCURATELY as possible. If need be, find a polite way to ask the signer to maybe have their pet in another room so you both can focus on the documents without distraction.

Big Two: LACK OF CLEANLINESS!

Now this is a big one! There will be times when you come into stunning, immaculate homes that are as clean as can be and then there will be homes that you walk into and do not want to touch a single thing except for the doorknob to leave. I have been in filthy homes, with visible bugs and still managed to maintain my pleasant demeanor and complete my signing.

One client I had a few years back had a ladybug infestation. I mean, they were EVERYWHERE! I do not do bugs under any circumstances, however I was able to keep my composure and had the client sign while I remained standing, keeping watch over my shoulder for any unwelcomed guest trying to hitch a ride home with me.

You are allowed to stand instead of sitting at a client's home. If the client offers you a seat or ask why you are standing, simply offer my response, "Oh no, its okay. I prefer to stand as I drive ALLLL day, so any opportunity I get to stand is welcomed." *SMILE*

When dealing with house that can use a deep clean, remain pleasant and focus on completing the documents in a quick and ACCURATE fashion. If you are offered a drink, simply reply with "Oh Thank you but I just had lunch. I am stuffed," or "Oh no, that's okay, I have a water bottle in the car that I am working on. Thank you, though." Remember to SMILE!

BIG THREE: THE SIGNERS & THEIR FAMILY

People are all different in personality and temperaments so you will come across those who are not as pleasant as you are. There have been times where they clients themselves have been disrespectful and rude in which case I remain polite and simply ask if the client would like to continue. If they say yes, then I finish as quickly as possible without appearing to be intentional in rushing to leave. If they say no, which has never happened to me unless the loan documents themselves were wrong, then you simply let the hiring company know what happened after you leave their home.

There have been instances where the other people in the house, including the clients were arguing amongst each other. I have even witnessed a fight during a closing. You see a little bit of everything in this line of work. Simply remain poised and polite and excuse yourself if the situation is too uncomfortable for you and let the hiring company know what happened.

I was headed to client's house for a loan signing once and upon arrival I realized there was a shooting that had taken place maybe a few minutes before and there were swarms of police cars on that block that appeared to be running around trying to find the shooter. So yes, I did make a U-Turn and take myself back home. On the ride home, I called the client who completely understood and repeatedly apologized, and I also called the hiring company who agreed that my safety was way more important.

Never put yourself in a situation that you do not feel comfortable with. With that being said, I know several notary/signing agents that do carry firearms with them especially when they are meeting people after hours. As far as bringing firearms into people's homes (concealed of course), that is a shade of grey that you will have decide on for yourself.

You do have a job to do but you want to make sure you are keeping yourself safe as well. Be sure if you meet someone that is not a client conducting a loan closing that you meet at a public place if it is after hours like a Panera or McDonalds. Safety First, Signing Second!

REGISTER TODAY FOR NOTARY2NOTARY ONLINE TRAINING

There are several trainings that teach notaries how to build their businesses focused around loan closings. What separates Notary2Notary from the others is that we focus on building your notary business in more areas than simply loan closings. Our online course (www.notary2notary.com/thinkific.com) , YouTube Channel and In-Person Trainings/Live Webinars teach how to successfully build your notary business within the following four tiers:

- GENERAL NOTARY WORK
- LOAN CLOSINGS

- E-NOTARY
- NON-NOTARY WORK

Our program is built around teaching notaries nationwide how to establish a successful notary business that can be worked as a full-time business. We pride ourselves in constant communications which is why we have weekly live webinars where students can ask real time questions. All webinars are available for replay as well.

As a thank you for purchasing this book, you can save $50 on any of our online training courses by using Promo Code: IREADIT.

HAPPY SIGNING!